Este Libro Pertenece A
This Book Belongs To

_____

Por Eden Hitchcock
Ilustraciones de Eden Hitchcock
Editado por Lisa Rinaldo

The House
By Eden Hitchcock
Illustrations by Eden Hitchcock
Edited by Lisa Rinaldo

Copyright 2019 PS Publishing
All rights reserved. Printed in the USA.
No part of this book may be reproduced or copied in any form without express written permission from the publisher.
ISBN: 978-1-942333-18-0

La Casa was selected as the 2019 Winner of the Books 4 Kids Write Across America contest!

Submissions were received from authors ranging in age from 5 to 15! Eden was just eight years old when she signed a publishing contract with PS Publishing. *La Casa* was chosen, among dozens of contestants, for its creative way of offering a bi-lingual story of acceptance in a very non-conventional way.

This story was written in Spanish and translated to English for early elementary students.

Hay diferentes tipos de lugares donde vivimos.

There are different places where we live.

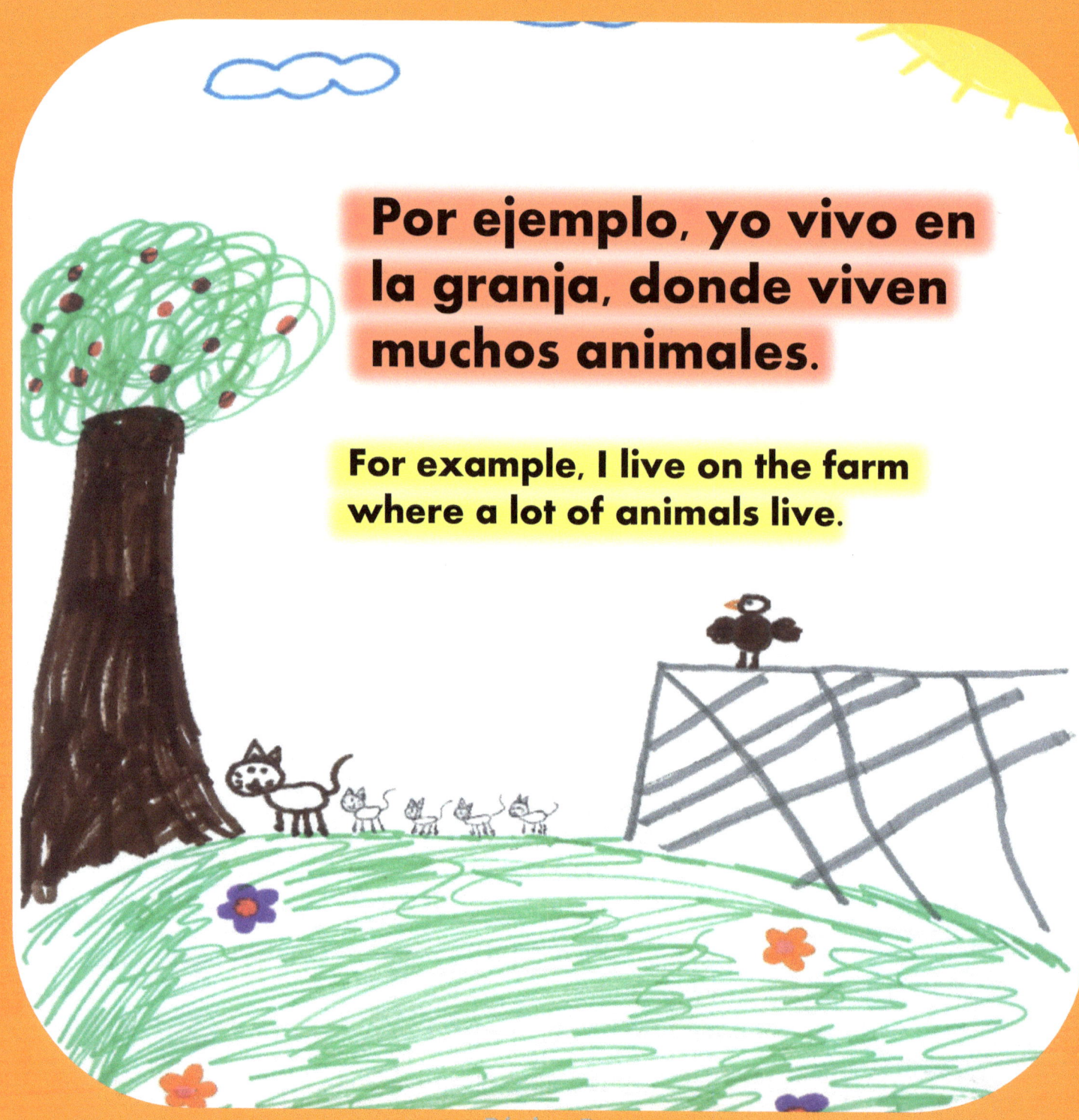

Otras personas viven en la ciudad donde hay mucho ruido.

Other people live in the city where there is a lot of noise.

Otras personas viven en lugares con casitas y no mucho ruido. Porque estan lejos de la ciudda.

Other people live in places with little houses and not much noise because they are far from the city.

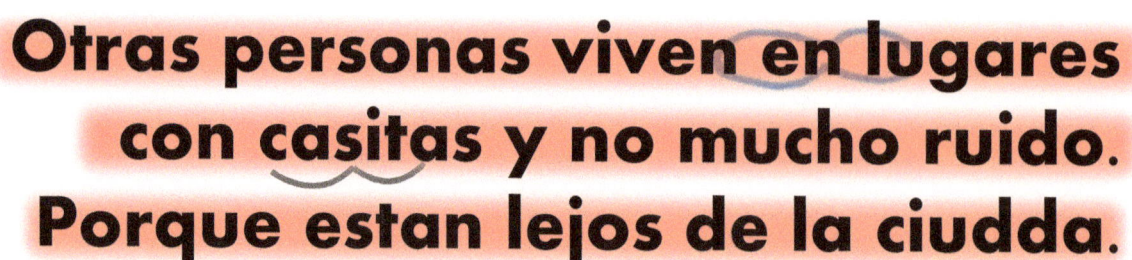

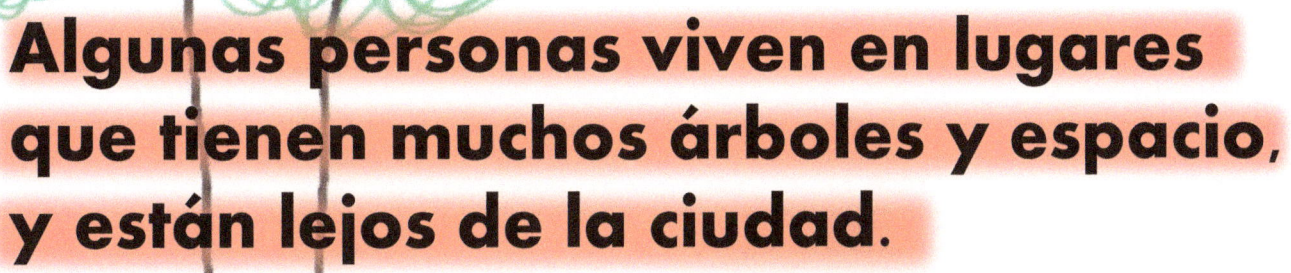

Algunas personas viven en lugares que tienen muchos árboles y espacio, y están lejos de la ciudad.

Some people live in places that have lots of trees and space, and is far from the city.

¿**Dónde vives tu**?

Where do you live?

¿Vives cerca o lejos de otras casas?

Do you live near or far from other houses?

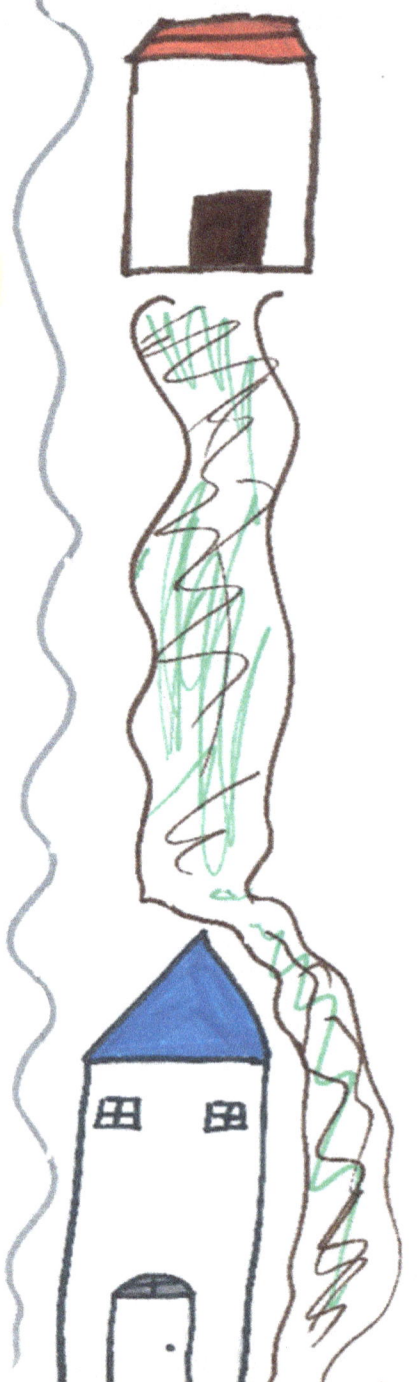

¿Tienes un vecino?

Do you have a neighbor?

Pero no importa nada de eso,

But none of that is important,

Porque lo más importante es que ...

Because the most important thing is...

te gusta donde vives,

that you like where you live,

Jugar,

play,

aprender,

learn,

Y donde itienes un buen dia!

and where you have a good day!

Sobre el Autor

Eden Hitchcock es un estudiante de inmersión en español en Sonia Sotomayor Elementary en Sioux Falls, South Dakota. Además de escribir, le encanta hacer tiendas imaginarias y criar conejos. Fue autora e ilustró este libro a los ocho años.

About the author

Eden Hitchcock is a Spanish immersion student at Sonia Sotomayor Elementary in Sioux Falls, South Dakota. Besides writing, she loves making pretend stores and raising rabbits. She authored and illustrated this book at age eight.

Sonia Sotomayor Elementary

The following information can be found on the school website:

"Since 2008, the Sioux Falls School District Spanish Immersion Program has been teaching native English speaking students a second language by immersing them in a classroom with a Spanish speaking teacher. All of the classroom instruction occurs in Spanish beginning in kindergarten. Students read, write, and speak Spanish as they go through their daily lessons. Students learn through the same curriculum as students in a traditional English classroom in the Sioux Falls School District, however the curriculum is in Spanish.

Sonia Sotomayor has an enrollment of 560 students in kindergarten-5th grade and 34 students in our Mis Amigos Learning Adventures Preschool.

The staff at Sonia Sotomayor represent 18 different countries and provide students with a wide variety of cultural experiences!"

Educator Jenny Egstad encouraged Eden to submit her story to the Books 4 Kids writing contest, and we're so glad she did. Thank you Ms. Egstad and everyone at Sonia Sotomayor Elementary!

BOOKS 4 KIDS PROGRAM

The Books 4 Kids Program is a grass-roots 501c3 program founded in South Dakota. B4K's mission is: "Building Children's Character Through Books, and Their Confidence Through Inclusion."

When we send our children to pre-school, they love each other. Then the book fair comes to town and divides the children into "haves" and "have-nots."

Rather than using books to divide classmates, the Books 4 Kids Program uses books to bring students together.

Books 4 Kids events bring authors into the classroom—usually electronically. The author reads with the students and, whenever possible, leads a student discussion about the book, the weather, or whatever the student asks. At the end of the session, every student receives a copy of the book for free!

So how does that bring students together? From meeting the author to receiving a book, B4K starts conversations. When you have students on opposite ends of a spectrum—whether it be financial, academic or physical—what do they have in common? In some cases, their Books 4 Kids Program event is their only common denominator.

In addition to the positive impacts B4K has on bringing students together, each story contains an age-appropriate, character-building lesson. B4K includes a book on empathy toward animals that teaches early readers animals have feelings. Other lessons in Books 4 Kids stories include: bullying, respect for others, friendship, work-ethic, self-esteem and cyber-bullying.

The Books 4 Kids Program is a 501c3 non-profit that operates entirely on the generosity of sponsors.

If you would like to support B4K with a tax-deductible gift visit www.B4Kprogram.org

@Books4KidsProgram

@Books4KidsProgram

www.ingramcontent.com/pod-product-compliance
Lightning Source LLC
Chambersburg PA
CBHW040007080526
44586CB00027B/2908